James Leach

Rachel

Christmas 1989.

Stiffkey.

If you enjoy reading about Norfolk and Suffolk, Cambridgeshire and Essex, look for titles from 'Poppyland Publishing'

Available at the time of printing: The 'East Anglian Memories' series

Those Seaside Days
When Wherries Sailed By

The 'Albums' series

The Rows of Yarmouth
A Mundesley Album
A Cromer Album
A Sheringham Album
Poppyland in Pictures

The 'Norfolk Origins' series

Hunters to First Farmers
Roads and Tracks
Celtic Fire and Roman Rule

Town and Village History Booklets

East and West Runton — Two Villages, One Parish
Great Yarmouth — History, Herrings and Holidays
Cley — Living with Memories of Greatness
Caister — 2000 Years a Village
Have You Heard about Blakeney?
Poppyland — Strands of Norfolk History
Palling — A History Shaped by the Sea
Coltishall — Heyday of a Broadland Village
Salthouse — Village of Character and History
Cromer — The Chronicle of a Watering Place
Potter Heigham — The Heart of Broadland
An Acle Chronicle

Lifeboat Histories

The Gorleston Volunteer Lifeboat 'Elizabeth Simpson'
Ther Hunstanton Lifeboats
Caister — Beach Boats and Beachmen
The Cromer Lifeboats

Miscellaneous Titles

Norwich at War
Coastal Towns at War
Great Yarmouth at War
Arthur Ransome's East Anglia
'Skipper' Jack
East Anglia on Film
His Majesty's Late Ship the Invincible
Taking the Children Too...
The Birds of Sheringham
Aylsham in the 17th Century
Sounds of North Norfolk (audio-cassette)

Many more titles are in preparation. For a current list, ask at your bookshop or write to Poppyland Publishing, 13, Kings Arms Street, North Walsham Norfolk NR28 9JX

FOR DAVID, MARK AND GUY

© Sheila Woods 1989
Design and Layout by Top Floor Design
Typesetting by PTPS
Printed by Printing Services (Norwich) Ltd
Published by Poppyland Publishing, North Walsham, Norfolk
First Published 1989
ISBN 0 94614842 2

OUT WITH THE TIDE

Recollections of Wells-next-the-Sea

Sheila Woods

The 'East Anglian Memories' series

FOREWORD

 "Out with the Tide" is not intended to be a guide, neither is it a history; it is an account of life in the town of Wells-next-the-Sea in the eventful year of 1939, seen through the naive eyes of an 11 year old. Memory, however, is a very personal thing and others will have different memories. These are mine.

The outbreak of war in September, 1939, marked the end of a way of life in many small towns and villages throughout the country, but perhaps more so in Norfolk than in some areas, as that county was destined to change from a strictly rural, agricultural area into a training ground for the armed forces and home for thousands of servicemen, many of whom came from very different surroundings. Small communities, such as Wells, hitherto complete in themselves, were now playing host to outsiders, who inevitably brought change.

The war itself brought changes which, although they would have occurred eventually, would not have arrived so soon. Because of the need for food to be grown at home, agriculture became more important to the country and new methods were introduced which changed the nature of farming. Tractors replaced horses, scythes and binders were superseded by combine harvesters and hedges were uprooted to form even larger fields, whilst small farms were swallowed up in larger ones. The pre-war way of farming disappeared for ever, and, alas, many skills with it.

It was not only the boats that went *"Out with the Tide"* in Wells; the old way of life went out with the tide of progress.

Sheila Woods

I should like to express my gratitude to Mr David Cox, BEM, former coxswain of the Wells lifeboat, for all the help he gave me with information on the lifeboat and the fishing industry.

SW

PART 1

SPRING AND
SUMMER 1939

The west end of the Quay, early in the century.

CHAPTER ONE

 "*Shut the door*" called my mother. "*The wind's in the north-east!*"

The wind always seemed to be in the north-east since we had come to live in the new house. Previously we had lived in Park Road in one of a row of terraced cottages, with a garden snugly enclosed by a high fence, turning it into a suntrap. The new house was one of a little crescent of eight solidly built red brick semi-detached houses with pantiled roofs, standing on a hill about 200 yards from the shoreline. The straight flint wall running the length of the road in front of the houses was probably the site of a rope walk known to have existed at this end of the town, while the garden space at the back looked out past allotments to cornfields, which stretched as far as the eye could see, parallel with the salt marshes which edge that part of the North Norfolk coast. The north-east wind blew in from the sea across the marshes and shrivelled everything in its path. Now, in March, it was at its most vicious. My mother was fond of saying that there was no more mainland between our back door and the North Pole. Whether or not this was true, it certainly felt like it.

We had only recently moved to the east end of the town. There had been many visits while the house was being constructed and then the interminable wait while it had been left to "dry out", but at last the great day had arrived and we were to move.

I had fully expected to be let off school and share in the excitement. To me the move seemed comparable with the American wagons going west. My father arrived with Duke harnessed to a farm wagon and I was prepared to roll eastwards through the town to start a new life, but to my disgust I was sent off to school as usual with the injunction "*Don't forget to come home to the new house.*" By the time I arrived everything was in place. There was really nothing to moving after all. The new house bristled with modern conveniences; no longer would water have to be fetched from a pump in the yard, but appeared on demand at the flick of a wrist; my mother now had the advantage of a gas stove whose heat she could control, and had bade farewell to the temperamental black-leaded kitchen range which pleased itself more than it did her. But best of all electricity replaced the oil lamps and candles of before, which meant that reading in bed could no longer be condemned as a dangerous occupation.

My bedroom window looked out across the fields and on a clear day the twin towers of Blakeney church, seven miles away, were visible. The road in front of the house continued downhill between fishermen's cottages to the shore line, close by the spot where boats had once been built. Oyster smacks had been built here for local use, but boat building had ceased around the end of the nineteenth century and now all that remained were two slipways leading down into the sea, and the name on the adjacent pub *"The Shipwrights Arms"*.

The town of Wells-next-the-Sea with its harbour, stands on a tidal estuary more than a mile from the open sea. Here, at the east end of the town the harbour channel diminishes to a tidal creek deep with mud at low tide and flanked to the north by salt marshes. The creek divides into tributaries which wind through the marshes, sometimes petering out in the mud, but which fill swiftly with the incoming tide and at the season of the highest tides water covers the marshes completely, giving the appearance to the town of being on the edge of the open sea.

The shore at this end of the town lies thick with oyster and mussel shells. Mussels had been gathered here in former years, but the beds had been poisoned by the town's sewage which had been discharged straight into the water in the harbour at high tide. Today fresh, unpolluted mussel lays exist further into the creek.

The former Primary School at Wells. Photo: Mark Woods

The plaque on the old Primary School at Wells. Photo: Mark Woods   •

On this cold spring day I had plenty to tell my mother on returning from school. It had been *"Scholarship Day"*, the day on which the children in the top class of the Primary School sat the examination which determined which school they would attend next. Like many of the older buildings in the town the school was built of the local grey flint and intended to last for ever. On one of the outside walls, about two thirds of the way up the single storey building, was a flat stone plaque announcing that this was a British School built with the aid of the Countess of Leicester. This plaque was very popular in the ball season as it was the only place on the flint walls flat enough against which to bounce a ball. There was a definite season for playing with balls, another for skipping ropes and another for marbles. There was no fixed date for the change from one form of game to another, but suddenly everyone would know it was time for a change and no-one played ball in the skipping season, or brought a skipping rope to school in the marbles season.

But today no-one's thoughts had been on games. *"The Scholarship"* was the climax of all the years spent at the Primary School. We had been coached on what to expect for weeks beforehand and now the day of reckoning had arrived. There had been two papers to complete, first an English paper and then Arithmetic. We had been told to make a note of our answers to the sums on our blotting paper and in the afternoon the teacher had checked the answers.

I had great news to tell.

"Mum, if I've done as well in English as I have in Arithmetic I'll be all right. I got all my sums right."

My mother was delighted, but a sterner critic was at hand. My aunt had been visiting my mother when I arrived home. Both her sons had passed the examination and gone on to the Grammar School at Fakenham, ten miles away.

"If it was that easy" she said, *"a lot of you will have passed. That means the oral exam will be extra difficult to weed some of you out."*

Visions of the coveted maroon and gold hatband and blazer receded. The wind was definitely in the north east.

The next six weeks passed very slowly as we waited for the results to be announced. My mother did her best to convince me that the world would not come to an end if I didn't pass the exam but I wanted to pass very badly. My two cousins had both passed the exam and the elder was going to University in the autumn. I wasn't at all sure where University was, but I gathered that it was a very desirable place to go and that it was somewhere in the region of Nottingham.

At last the results of the written exam arrived. Seven of us had passed. The next hurdle was the oral exam which had to be taken at the Grammar School itself.

Fakenham is a small market town some ten miles from Wells. To get to the school entailed a 20 minute journey by train and then a walk of about a mile to the school itself, which was at the far end of the town. The school had originally been an early nineteenth century yellow brick house called *"Highfields"*, to which extra wings and buildings had been added as the school grew. It was built on land which we were told by the history mistress had once belonged to John o'Gaunt, and the school had adopted his *"fleur de lys"* as their crest. We made our way through the town in a solemn little group, huddled together for confidence, and very conscious of the issues which were at stake. The school appeared awesomely in front of us at the top of a hill. With its laboratories, craft rooms and gymnasium grouped round a quadrangle, it bore as much relation to our single storeyed primary school as a cathedral to a village church. Somehow or other I had to gain admittance to this wonderland. I knew that at the Grammar School I could read Shakespeare and learn French, both of which I was very anxious to do. Wells had very little to offer a girl in the way of employment except shop work, and I felt that to learn another language would be the first step to a more exciting life in the outside world. Shakespeare was something I had already had a glimpse of in poetry books. I sensed the magic of the words, which were satisfyingly difficult, but this was obviously a challenge with which I would need help.

The oral exam itself was very brief. We were ushered, one by one, into what I later discovered to be the library, and confronted with three serious gentlemen in grey suits, with uncomfortable starched shirt collars, which made them sit very upright. They asked me questions about myself and what I liked doing at school, and then told me a story about a horse and asked what was wrong with the story. The answer was so obvious I couldn't believe it could be so easy. I considered carefully, looking for a more complicated reason. As a farmer's daughter who had been brought up with horses, I couldn't conceive of anyone making such an elementary mistake, but I could find no other answer and hesitatingly gave my opinion. *"That's right"* they said, and I left the room in astonished relief.

The tension lifted, we dawdled our way back to the railway station, relishing our freedom, but not one of us anxious to discuss our performance. We left the shops behind and entered the long straight road to the railway station. From the trees beside the road a cuckoo called.

"Did you hear that?" said J. *"Which side of us was he on?"*

"What difference does it make?" we said.

"But it does." said J. *"Listen."*

We listened, and the cuckoo called again.

"It's to the right of us" said J excitedly. *"That means we shall come back to this place."*

And in September we did. To my delight I had been awarded a scholarship.

My mother's friends were very enthusiastic. *"She'll make a good little teacher,"* they said.

But I wasn't so sure. To be a teacher would mean wearing my hair in a bun, and it might not suit me. Besides, I might want to be something else.

A sailor's gravestone in Wells churchyard. Photo: Mark Woods

CHAPTER TWO

 The world outside was concerned with greater issues. Everywhere the talk was of war. Would there be one, or not? Grave faced knots of people stood outside their houses in the evenings reminding themselves about *"the last one"* and how expensive food had been, and how difficult it had been to get eggs. I wasn't too concerned. I didn't like eggs much anyway. But the anxiety was apparent everywhere and wouldn't go away. For me, war meant anonymous men in uniforms fighting battles in some conveniently distant country. As the gloom deepened I began to feel that if it was going to upset everyone so by having the threat hanging over our heads, perhaps it would be best to have a war and get it over with and then everyone could be happy again.

My father had volunteered to become an Air Raid warden. In the event of an air raid he was to get on his bicycle and ride round our part of the town turning off all the gas street lamps with a long pole . When war eventually came the lamps were no longer lit, so his speed was never really tested.

At school, on the other hand, now that the examination was over, tension had slackened. My way home led me past the house of one of the teachers who had a number of cats. Every morning, after the school milk had been distributed, my job was to pour all the dregs left into a jam jar which I carried to the teacher's house on my way home. I took pride in this responsibility and was referred to as *"the cats' friend"*.

Summer afternoons at school were spent in practising country dancing for displays which were given at various garden fetes held in the town. In addition to the Parish Church, there was a Congregational chapel, a Methodist chapel, a Wesleyan chapel and a Friends Meeting House. Each of them held a garden fete to raise funds during the summer and as most people attended some place of worship everyone had a turn at helping run their particular event. The fetes were held at the same four or five houses in the town each year. These were houses which were large enough to have gardens for pleasure with lawns and open spaces. The majority of gardens in the town were for the strictly practical purpose of providing food and every inch was devoted to this. Trees were only to be seen if they provided fruit and ornamental shrubs were rare indeed. The fetes were identical and the only way of telling which organisation was running the event was by identifying the people manning the stalls and their usual place of worship. And we all knew this anyway. The fete would be opened by the owner of the house and garden, who would then invite us to patronise the stalls arranged in a semi-circle round the edge of the lawn. These contained handmade garments and knitted goods, secondhand clothes and a white elephant stall. On this could be found odd bits of Victorian jewellery, thought only suitable for children for *"dressing up"*, empty picture frames, vases and odd bits of china. I spent much thought on which frame would best suit my precious photograph of Ginger Rogers and Fred Astaire cut from the newspaper. The bran tub usually had three different sorts of *"surprises"*. The trick was to stand and watch until we had seen all three drawn out and unwrapped and then we knew which shape to feel for. Teas were supplied on card tables near the house and the climax of the event was the display of dancing given by the schoolchildren.

This year, after the dancing, the owner of the house came up to me and to my amazement said *"I hear you've just won a scholarship. Get yourself an ice-cream"*. He put twopence into my hand. He was the local doctor and I had always had a great respect for him since, several years earlier, he had cured my teddy bear. At the age of five I had had a series of illnesses which had kept me in bed for three months. The doctor had visited frequently and one day, tired of having nothing to do but look at the drawn curtains, I produced my teddy bear from under the sheet and asked if he could cure it. Teddy had lost one eye. The doctor examined the bear gravely, placing his stethoscope to his chest, but said he feared he could do nothing as it was a hospital case. Bitterly disappointed I returned Teddy to the bed. However on his next visit the doctor enquired if I thought Teddy was fit to travel as Matron at the hospital had told him she had an empty bed. Fearfully I handed over the bear and awaited developments. The next week's visit arrived at last and the doctor returned with my teddy bear, his head swathed in bandages. On removing the bandages I found he had indeed been cured of his blindness having had a new eye fitted. Now this worker of miracles had given me twopence for an ice-cream. I had never had a twopenny ice-cream before. My usual purchase was a halfpenny cornet and on special days, such as birthdays, I might have a penny wafer, but never had I had a twopenny wafer. Would I be able to eat it all? I did.

The ice-cream man was only one of the people delivering in the streets. He, being a modern innovation, had a tricycle with a large container on the front in which the ice-cream was kept. He wore a white coat and peaked cap and his ringing bell was a constant invitation to *"Stop me and buy one"*.

Most things were delivered to the door, and frequently horses provided the power. There was no shortage of fish on the coast and some people preferred to collect their shellfish free from the beach, where the winkles could be found clinging to the stones at low tide and cockles betrayed their presence by a hole in the wet sand. But the fishmonger's cart still did a brisk trade and his cry of *"Fish-O"* was one of the earliest to be heard in the streets in the mornings.

Coal was delivered to the houses by horse, and cart and anything else which had to be moved was carried in the same way. The lighter goods, however, were pushed in handcarts. The baker sent out his bread in a basket work handcart which was pushed by a boy only 3 years older than myself, who had just left school. The postman made one delivery on foot with the letters and then returned with a handcart, this time painted post office red, to deliver the parcels. The cart containing the parcels could be left quite safely in the road while the postman disappeared round the back of a house with a parcel. No-one would have dreamed of tampering with the Royal Mail and anyone thought guilty of stealing would have become a social outcast. The Ten Commandments were not only taught very thoroughly at school but people were expected to live their lives by them. And most did.

A visit from the telegraph boy, on the other hand, was dreaded. The belief that he only brought news of death probably had some foundation, as with few telephones in the town, this was the most common reason for an urgent communication.

The milk was delivered in churns from a pony and trap. His approach was easily recognisable from the jingling bells on the horse's harness. The milkman was a favourite of mine. He was the father of one of my friends and before I was old enough to go to school I would stand at the door with my mother waiting for his arrival and clutching the milk jug from my doll's teaset. He never failed to fill my jug first.

A common visitor to the town was the organ-grinder with his monkey. The man was short and swarthy with a stained suit and greasy trilby hat. Round his neck was a spotted handkerchief and the lugubrious expression he wore went ill with the gaiety of his tunes. The monkey wore a little red jacket and pillbox hat and was tethered by a chain attached to a collar round his neck. His usual pitch was halfway down Staithe Street and the monkey would run to the extent of his chain with a collecting box, scratching himself enthusiastically. I could not understand why my mother, who was normally so generous, would not allow me to approach the monkey to put a penny in his box and even insisted that I watch from the other side of the street. Where he came from and where he went I do not know. He had always

The memorial to the crew of the lifeboat 'Eliza Adams'. Photo: Mark Woods

disappeared by the next day.

The town had its quota of home-grown characters too. At the west end of the Quay, near the memorial to the men who had been lost in the lifeboat *"Eliza Adams"*, an old mast had been propped horizontally to form a seat. This was usually occupied by seafaring elder statesmen who still wore their fishermen's jerseys or slops and mardled the day away while keeping a watchful eye seawards. None of them actually had a wooden leg or carried a parrot perched on his shoulder, which was disappointing, but to me they were Long John Silver and Sinbad rolled into one. I imagined conversations of *"ivory, apes and peacocks"*. The idea that they were more likely to be discussing the *Canaries* last match was not one which would have occurred to me.

The 1836 Directory of Norfolk mentions that there were then 67 vessels registered as belonging to the port of Wells. In 1939 all boats bore the registration LN for King's Lynn and still do today. In 1836 there were yearly races held and a fair on Shrove Tuesday, but by 1939 these had been discontinued. There was also workhouse accommodation for 60-80 paupers at the earlier date, but the workhouse seldom held more than 40. Whether this meant that the people of Wells were too affluent to need all the accommodation, or whether they preferred any hardships to entry to the workhouse, is not made clear. There are also 26 public houses listed in 1836 as well as some half a dozen beer houses, of which 9 remained in 1939 with 2 more recent additions. In 1939 Whalebone Yard was still entered through the jawbone of a whale.

Among the older people there were three answers to the question *"How are you?"*. The answer was *"Nicely thank you"*, *"I'm fairly, you know"* or *"I'm poorly"*. The first meant they were feeling very well, the second that they were not feeling well but had no intention of going into the details as there was nothing you could do anyway, but the third meant that they needed sympathy.

The focal point of the town was the Quay. From there three streets or roads ran at right angles back to one road running parallel to the coast road and then continued to a third parallel road at the southern, inland edge of the town. In between the three main thoroughfares were numerous lanes, alleys and yards lined with maltings at the northernmost end nearest to the Quay, but becoming inhabited further into the town. Many of the older houses and cottages were made of the local flint and those in terraces were often joined all along the row through their attics so that if Excise men came to call, any smugglers could escape further along the row. The maltings were grim looking buildings. Built of brick, some four or five storeys high and

Favor Parker's granary and the Old Maltings. Photo: Mark Woods

sometimes coated with tar, they were forbidding and mysterious. Their slatted windows prevented any glimpse of the malting process of the barley but the swinging cowls on their chimneys emitted a dank fusty smell which hung over the town like an over-ripe cloud.

The Quay itself was lined with granaries. These were equally tall, brick built buildings, without the cowled chimneys, but with a covered hoist at one side. Their windows were often covered with shutters with a round hole in the middle through which well fed pigeons flew in and out at will. On asking why there should be holes which allowed birds to steal the grain, it was suggested that the holes were there to allow cats in to catch the rats! I imagined the battles to the death which must take place and hoped someone washed the grain at some stage.

Local people were drawn to the Quayside as if by a magnet at high tide. This was always the time of most activity, with cargo boats entering or leaving the harbour and the arrival or departure of the whelk boats.

The sea warms more slowly than the land, but by June local boys would be diving off the Quay at high tide and swimming in the deep water. At low tide the water retreats along the channel past the beach to the open sea, until in some places it is possible to walk on the mud under the Quay wall, leaving any cargo boats in the harbour aground. But the tide comes in swiftly and treacherously, lifting the boats off the bottom and filling the harbour. It was then that the boys would swim,

The hoist on the granary, now removed with the conversion of the building for other purposes. Photo: Mark Woods

some standing and diving rather self-consciously, for there was usually an admiring crowd, and some running straight off the wall and entering the water feet first. Some would swim under water for quite a distance before surfacing, and non-swimmer that I was, I would hold my breath fearfully until they reappeared. But however they entered the water they always swam when the tide was coming in, and then only to the seaward side of the sewage outlets!

A variety of types of fishing boat, including whelkers and flat bottomed mussel boats, at the east end of Wells harbour in the years prior to the war.

The Quay from the west, early in the century. In the background railway wagons stand at the quayside.

CHAPTER THREE

One of the main industries of the town was fishing for whelks. These were sent to markets in Birmingham and all over the North-East as well as to Billingsgate. The whelkhouses were situated at the east end of the town past the main harbour, where an extension of the railway line from the station looped round the edge of the town to pass the whelkhouses and then continued along to the Quay itself. An engine shunted wagons as far as the whelkhouses, but after this those continuing on to the Quay were harnessed to three horses who pulled them along the lines.

The fishing fleet left with the tide in the morning and returned with the incoming tide in the evening. The boats were often owned and operated by members of the same family, one remaining behind to light the coppers to boil the catch on their return. The boats were deep, sturdy and clinker built, some 26 to 30 feet long and were built at Sheringham. They still carried a sail but by now relied on engines as well. There was no shelter in the boats apart from a small cuddy in the bows. The outward trip to the fishing ground, 10 miles off, took about an hour in 1939, but today the grounds have moved and the outward and return trips take three hours each. Each boat carried 240 pots, each attached to 90 feet of rope which were baited with herring and bits of codfish and left behind when the boats returned. On the next trip all these pots had to be lifted, emptied and rebaited before being returned to the water, to await the next trip. Smoke belching from the chimneys of the whelkhouses announced to the rest of the town that the boats were on their way back. The coal-fired coppers held 30-40 gallons and were the centre of activity inside the whelkhouses. The unloading of the boats was a long and arduous business, the whelks being carried in nets from yokes, two bushels at a time, from the boat, across the shore to the whelkhouse which was lit by the glare of the coppers. The whole area had a smell all its own, made up of a mixture of tarred rope, the boiling whelks, and ash, which had been scattered on what passed for a road. When the boiling went on into the evening the light would escape from the roofs through gaps between the tiles sending dozens of small searchlights up into the sky. When the whelks had been boiled they would be emptied into hessian sacks ready for despatch by train. Today the whelks are processed, frozen and packed in a factory in the town itself.

In the summer of 1940 a signal arrived from the Admiralty, Northern Command, for all available fishing boats to proceed to Ramsgate, although no reason was given for the order. The boats leaving from Wells were

Rose with Mr C. Grimes, Mr R Grimes and Mr J Barnes
Mal Vina with Mr D Cooper, and Mr R Cringle
Bessie with Mr C Stephenson, Mr W Cox and Mr L Cox
Tony with Mr T Neilsen, Mr A Powditch and Mr J Youngman
Q J J with Mr S Cooper and Mr W Whitaker
Little Admiral with Mr D Pegg and Mr T Pegg
Ace with Mr C Jarvis and Mr E Jarvis

They were joined by a boat from Brancaster, one from Blakeney and some fishermen from Sheringham.

The journey to Ramsgate took several days and when the boats arrived, the evacuation from Dunkirk, which had been the reason for the order, was practically completed. Only *Rose* actually made the crossing.

The whelk house, when the tide is out. Photo: Mark Woods

CHAPTER FOUR

 The high point of the Summer was the town's Regatta and Carnival when the town showed itself off to outsiders who crowded in from the trains all day from several miles around. The station itself was a terminus of the London and North Eastern line, with one line running south to Norwich through Fakenham and Dereham and the other running along the coast to Heacham, where there were connections for King's Lynn. As there were stations at every village along the way, transport was no problem. In addition buses ran along the coast in the other direction through Stiffkey and Blakeney to Sheringham and Cromer.

The first news of the Regatta, or any other event, would be delivered by the Town Crier, and several weeks before the actual Regatta Day a special dance would be held at which the Carnival Queen would be chosen. Entry was restricted to local girls and there was much partisan speculation as to who would wear the crown and who would be in attendance. The Town Crier wore no special costume, but the summons of his bell and the tremendous power of his voice ensured that everyone would be at their doors to listen from the very first *"Oyez"*. He stopped at each corner throughout the town and proclaimed his message *'Oyez, oyez, A-dance-will-be-held-in-the-Church-room- on-Saturday -1st-August -at-8pm- to- choose-the- Carnival -Queen-admission- 1/6d. Oyez, oyez"*. The whole message was delivered on one note, but with the force of a battering ram. In between proclamations he rang his bell vigorously and continuously. There was no excuse for being uninformed.

The date of the Regatta has always been governed by the time of the tide, but took place, about the second Saturday in August. The event was something to savour for weeks beforehand. Pocket money had to be saved to spend at the Fair, costumes had to be prepared for the Carnival and impatience had to be contained. As the great day approached the streets and houses would sprout flags and bunting, and individual shops would be brightened with flowers for the best decorated shop competition. There was also a best decorated house competition and curtains would be washed and window boxes refurbished while facades disappeared beneath banners proclaiming *"Success to our Regatta"*.

A high proportion of the 3,000 population participated in some way in the day's events, but being a non-swimmer, my activities were confined to the Carnival. The procession assembled at the Buttlands at 2 p.m. for the judging, before parading through the town. The Buttlands, which the name implies was once used for archery practice, was a pleasant grass area surrounded by mature Lime trees with a bandstand in the centre, occupied by the town band, which played until it was time to lead the procession. We assembled in our special classes, according to age, or method of transport. Most were on foot, but there were a few tradesmen's decorated vehicles, and of course, the lorry for the Queen and her attendants. There was usually a good assortment of clowns, fairies, queens of hearts and nursery rhyme or *"topical"* characters. A friend and I had entered as *"The Bisto Kids"* but the judges were not impressed and passed us by, but we could be sure of a cheer when we passed the family along the route. Any controversial action on the part of the Urban District Council often provoked a comic entry, which was usually awarded a popular first prize. The judging over, we moved off to tour the town, led by the Queen and her attendants; the favoured ones wearing their prize badges and the rest of us enjoying the attention anyway. The streets would be packed with spectators impatiently peering round corners to see why it was taking so long, but as soon as the official car passed through the streets to clear the way and the band could be heard approaching, they settled back to laugh and cheer. The only unhappy people were the shopkeepers, forced to stay in their empty shops, while the rest of the town enjoyed itself.

The procession returning at last to the Buttlands, broke up as we all headed for the next part of the day's events, the sailing races and water sports. Those lining the streets would have to take their turn in the crowds to make the journey to the Quayside, but we in the procession could slip off in small groups and dart through the side alleys and arrive in time for a good place to view the events.

By the time the crowd reached the Quay the sharpies would be manoeuvring into position for the start of the first race, their white sails bearing the letter K and a number, dwarfed by the 180 degree arc of the Norfolk sky with its clear dazzling light. We waited eagerly for the starting gun, straining to see who had got off to a good start and who had been caught facing in the wrong direction.

The sailing dinghies having departed down the channel the water was clear for the rest of the water sports. There were rowing races, for two and four oars, when no-one could beat the fishermen, swimming races for all ages, races in barrels, diving from the Quay and, my personal favourite, the greasy pole. The well larded pole was suspended from the Quay wall and a succession of boys tried to walk, crawl or

A family boat trip from Wells in the 1930s.

dangle from it to reach the other end, but the variations in method were all equally unsuccessful and the only thing that was certain was that they would have to swim home. The judges for the water sports sat in sheltered style in a marquee erected on the salt marshes opposite the Quay wall, while we ordinary mortals braved the inevitable North-East wind. But the general excitement and air of gaiety kept our blood from freezing, and the sea lavender on the marshes, at its peak at this time of year, made a brave sight. Growing only along a few miles of the North Norfolk coast, in August the plants carpet the marshes with their flat sprays of delicate mauve flowers, suffering not at all by occasionally being covered by the sea at high tide. With the return of the sharpies and the presentation of cups and prizes the water sports ended, but the day was far from over for there was still the Fair to come.

The visit to the Fair in the evening was the highest pinnacle in a day of great heights, not least because it was one of the rare occasions when I was abroad after dark. Outlying members of the family gathered at our house in the evening, and we all set off together, father, mother, uncles, aunts and cousins.

The Fair called to us from afar as we hurried along the Quay to the dry marshes by the Beach Road where it was held. The noise and bustle, the shouting and laughter, the raucous mixture of tunes from the fairground organs, the flashing lights on the rides and the general air of gaiety and excitement were all so different from the usual sober, hardworking atmosphere of the town. It was a once a year experience.

The children's roundabouts were hand-propelled and boringly slow, but the adult rides were steam driven. Galloping horses with flaring nostrils and wild eyes and manes rose majestically up and down as they raced round to the deafening strains of *"Ma, he's making eyes at me"* quite easily drowning *"Red Sails in the Sunset"* on the children's rides. The Royal Hunt flashed by in pursuit of lions, tigers, leopards and ostriches, the shrieks of its riders competing with those of its whistle.

The Cake Walk did its best to dislocate every joint in our bodies, and to make sure that there was no chance of anyone wandering away into the darkness where they could not spend their money, the perimeter of the fair was marked by flaming torches stuck into the ground which roared and hissed alarmingly, their flames shooting three feet or more into the air.

There were stalls and sideshows which required skill and some which depended on chance. My father was a crack shot with a rifle and could win anything I fancied on the rifle range. He also considered it his right to win a coconut on the coconut shies and on the only occasion when he failed to do so there was no doubt in our minds that the nuts were unfairly fixed in the cups.

I was usually discouraged from trying my hand at darts, for the sake

Staithe Street circa 1920. Photo: Eric Reading collection.

of the general safety of the onlookers, but I enthusiastically rolled away my pennies towards squares designed to fit them so precisely that there was little hope of winning, and the money flowed unrelentingly inwards towards the stall holder. Hoopla looked so easy, but the rings landed tantalisingly askew on the stands displaying the coveted jewellery.

The rock stall was a source of wonder, with huge square sticks of rock in colours never seen in the local sweet shop, cut in pieces to display geometric and flower patterns in their centres. The stallholder greeted each customer personally with *"Hello my dear, how are you?"* thus guaranteeing herself a customer for life.

Back in the town the pubs were doing a roaring trade. Although they had now dwindled in number to about a dozen, this was enough to induce a fair amount of celebration in a population of just under 3,000. Several of the pubs were situated on the Quay, and although hundreds had stood there during the afternoon in perfect safety, it was to be expected that by closing time, or soon after, more than one would wander across the empty Quayside and straight over the Quay wall into the water. However, by then the tide would have gone out, so no great harm was done.

I have heard that in former times on Regatta night barrels of lighted tar were rolled down Staithe Street into the water. I was rather relieved that this had died out. The Regatta was quite exciting enough without barrels of burning tar.

The pump on Church Plain, the last public pump left in the town. The cell window of the old police station is in the background. Photo: Mark Woods

CHAPTER FIVE

 The end of the Summer brought the corn harvest. My father, together with his brother, was a tenant farmer of a smallholding about a mile outside the town, on the Holkham estate which was owned by a descendant of Coke of Norfolk who had initiated the crop rotation system. None of the smallholdings had farmhouses and the families lived in the town. At the centre of the estate was a park entirely surrounded by a flint and brick wall, which one of my great-grandfathers had helped to build.

The only habitation in the area was a gamekeeper's lodge, where my maternal grandfather was a gamekeeper on the estate, and it was here that my parents first met. My mother had returned to the lodge to nurse my grandmother who was ill, after having worked in London, and knew little of the tenants of the neighbouring farm save that they were two brothers, one of whom was named George. Imagine her horror on answering a knock at the door, to be greeted by a young man who said *"Please can you lend me a needle and thread, George has just cut his throat"*.

However, when he explained that he had a horse named George who had nicked his neck on some barbed wire, and in the absence of a vet he was about to perform some amateur surgery, she was much relieved.

There was no piped water in many of the houses in the town, so not surprisingly there was none on the farm either, and in the absence of any natural supply my father or uncle had to make the journey to Wells once a week to the pump by the church to fetch water in the water cart. This was a heavy rectangular iron cart with iron wheels which ground out deep ruts in the lanes. It was always pulled by Duke, the strongest of the three horses. He was a massive liver coloured Shire gelding with a white blaze on his forehead, feathered feet and hooves the size of dinner plates. He was the largest and strongest of the farm horses, but quiet as a lamb.

Not far from the pump was the blacksmith's forge, at the bottom of Market Lane. This was a good place to be in Winter and a fascinating place at any time of year. The smell of hot iron and burning horn, the showers of sparks springing up from the anvil and the stamping of the waiting horses, were all apparent long before the forge itself was entered. I had watched Duke being shod and hated to see the nails being hammered in, but my father was adamant that it didn't hurt and the horse certainly didn't seem to object. The sliding ring of horses' hooves on the roads was a common sound and there were quite as many horses about as cars. To own a car was very much the exception and not the rule.

Church Plain, Wells, in 1922. Photo: Eric Reading collection.

The farm was mainly used for arable purposes, but a few bullocks and a breeding sow, were kept. Round the farm buildings chickens roamed free roosting in the hedges and the wagon shed. I enjoyed searching the hedges for eggs and was delighted when my father suggested that I could call one of the hens my own. The birds were Rhode Island Reds and all looked alike to me, so I always had to ask my father which one of them was mine. I was amazed when it was always the one closest to us which my father identified and was delighted that the bird obviously knew me, and wanted to be friends.

Apart from the wagon shed, there was a large barn, a turnip house where the root crops were stored, a meal house which was always white and dusty and smelt strongly of the meal kept there, a cattle yard and shelter, a row of stables, pig styes, and *"the hut"* where my father and uncle consumed their mid-day sandwiches and cold tea with no milk or sugar, followed by a well deserved 40 winks. Farming with animals is a 365 day a year job and the stock had to be fed on Sundays, Christmas Day and any other Bank Holiday.

My father and uncle did all the work on the farm, except at harvest time when the whole family became involved in one way or another.

Mother feeding the pigs. The hat and gloves show that it is Sunday!

My boy cousins were old enough to do a day's work in the school holidays, but I was of little use except to deliver the tea and sandwiches for the *"Fourses"*, at first with my mother and later by myself. The journey to the farm by bicycle laden with heavy baskets and uphill all the way was tedious, but the journey back was a different matter. The lane had high hedges lined with pink convolvulus, their bases splashed with ox-eye daisies and poppies. Here the North-East wind could not penetrate and rushing downhill, zig-zagging to avoid the deep patches of silt ground out of the chalk by the farm wheels, was like flying through a tunnel of warm air. My cousins and I would race, scattering the chaffinches feasting on the seeds of the thistles which stood like sentinels at each gate we passed. But the boys were bigger and heavier than me, and their weight propelled their bikes faster and I always ended last.

Usually we ate the *"Fourses"* outside in the fields, making armchairs out of shocks of corn, but if rain was imminent, we ate in the barn. This had a hayloft at one end, which provided plenty of seating material and smelt strongly of the sacks of corn standing around. On nails on the walls hung all the farm implements; the scythes used for cutting the edges of the fields before the binder could get in, slashers for topping sugar beet, billhooks, saws, hammers and an axe, together with all the different forks. *"Doing a harvest"* was a popular way of earning pocket money for boys during the school holidays and there were usually one or two employed for a few weeks. Most of them worked hard, but if one was being a bit awkward my father would send him down to the blacksmith to ask for a *"skyhook"*. A mile's walk to the blacksmith and a shamefaced return uphill usually made its point.

There were no combine harvesters to gobble up the corn and digest it all in one operation, and very little farm machinery. Even tractors were rare and power was provided by horses. A great deal of skill was needed to time the cutting of the corn. Not only had the state of the crop to be judged, but the likelihood of rain in the ensuing days had to be decided so that, if possible, the corn could pass through the various stages from cutting to stacking in the dry. Humidity was also a great factor, for damp grain will heat and catch fire in the stack.

The author supervises as her father and uncle unharness the horses.

I loved the sense of order in the way the growing crop was transformed into a neat house-shaped stack, thatched and ready for
threshing.

The process began with my father and uncle mowing round the
outside of the field with scythes to make room for the binder to be
drawn in by Duke and the Percheron mare, Peggy. The wheat, barley
or oats would be scattered with thistles, poppies or delicate blue
scabious, which could not be eradicated from the soil as chemical
sprays were unknown, but which would wither and die long before the
grain was threshed. The horses would wear branches of elder in their
collars to keep off the flies, but still twitched and stamped impatiently
whenever they had to stand still. While these outside swathes were
being cut, my cousins and I, and all the other lads who would appear
whenever a field was due for cutting, would cut ourselves sticks from
the hedgerows with which to chase and kill rabbits, which were greatly
prized for rabbit pie and rabbit stew. When enough room had been
cleared and the binder had made its appearance, we formed ourselves
into an expectant ring round the standing corn. As the sails of the
binder gathered the corn and the bound sheaves were ejected, the
circle of hunters moved closer together ready to pounce on any rabbit
that decided to make a break for it. This had always seemed great sport
to me, although no rabbit had ever run across my path. Inevitably the
day arrived when one unhappy animal forced out of its cover ran
straight towards me. "*It's yours*" shouted my cousin. I raised my stick
automatically, but the creature looked terrified and I hurriedly put it
down again. My cousin sprinted over and quickly despatched the
rabbit, handing it to me. It was warm and soft and its eyes were wide
open. I dropped it in horror. It was the last time I joined the circle
round the corn.

If the weather was judged likely to hold, the sheaves were collected
from the lines where they had fallen and loaded up to be taken to be
stacked. The loading was done by pitchfork, one man throwing up the
sheaves on to the cart and another arranging them neatly inside. There
were usually two teams working in the field at once, Duke pulling the
tumbril and Peggy and Beauty, the Suffolk mare, pulling the wagon.
On arrival at the stack, which was accurately rectangular, the sheaves
would be again thrown up by pitchfork to the person standing on top.
If the weather was changeable, it would be necessary to place the
sheaves in shocks of eight before carting, ears uppermost, so that any
rain would run off them. When the house shaped stack had been
completed, it still had to be thatched, as it would be several weeks
before the contractor's steam driven traction engine arrived to thresh
the corn. This was the time when the hens were let into the fields to

gorge themselves on the dropped grain amongst the stubble.

All the fields had names, and this year disaster had come to "*Roundabouts*" and "*Bottom Five Acres*". "*Roundabouts*" enclosed "*Bottom Five Acres*" on three sides, hence its name, and these were the last fields to be harvested. The weather had been fine and the crops were heavy, but a violent storm had flattened the corn when it was too ripe to recover. The binder could not cope and as the corn harvest provided a great part of the year's income the loss of two whole fields would be disastrous. There was no alternative but for the whole family to glean. It was back-aching work, but necessity is a hard master. But if the work was hard, the conditions were very pleasant. The high hedges robbed the wind of much of its spite, and so long as we kept on to the end there was no-one to force the pace. Gradually we spread out and as the others became too far away for conversation, the stillness would reveal the rustle of an occasional harvest mouse trying to glean faster than we were. A bushel skep holds a great many ears of corn and any diversion was welcome, be it a solitary skylark ascending vertically into the endless Norfolk sky, or a rectangular flock of lapwings showing themselves first black and then white as they tilted against the sun.

Just before the end of the school holidays Hitler had marched into Poland. The final ultimatum had been ignored and war had been declared. Faces were grave, but life went on as usual in Wells.

Tomorrow was to be the first day at my new school and today it had rained since early morning. I thought of my new uniform already laid out on the bed and voiced my fears to my mother.

"*I hope it will be fine tomorrow*".

"*The rain will probably go out with the tide*" replied my mother.

PART TWO

AUTUMN AND WINTER

Wells-next-the-Sea locomotive depot in 1900. Railway wagons would be taken right down to the quayside for loading and unloading. Photo: Eric Reading collection.

The steam tug 'Marie' helps a vessel towards the bar, circa 1910. Photo: Eric Reading collection.

CHAPTER SIX

 The first day of term had arrived at last. Proudly wearing my new uniform and carrying a brand new satchel on one shoulder, and the hated gas-mask in its cardboard box on a piece of string on the other, I set off for the station. The rain had indeed gone out with the tide but the sun could not penetrate the heavy shade of the horse-chestnuts that lined the road to the railway station. Their leafy fingers were already preparing to plop their conkers straight down into our collections, but there was no time for conker gathering this morning. I suddenly felt very alone. The other new girls were already close friends and arrived together but none of my friends from the junior school were going on to Fakenham. The school train stood ready in the station, doors hanging open from half full carriages, and those who had started their journey from as far away as Burnham or Docking leaning out of windows anxious to be reunited with those they had not seen for the last seven weeks. I wandered up and down the platform wondering which carriage to enter. Many of the children I could not even recognise and those I could were engrossed in their own chattering groups. The engine hissed and whistled impatiently. At last the guard pointed to a door and said *"Come on, there's room in here"*. Grateful to have the decision made for me, I climbed into the carriage and sat down. No-one took any notice of me so I sat and listened. There was much talk of *"houses"* and *"fixtures"* and people whose nicknames evoked laughter. Then the conversation changed to the war. I had assumed that this was something that would take place at a convenient distance from me and have no direct influence on my life. But here was speculation as to whether we should all be sent to America. My sense of adventure dwindled. North Norfolk suddenly seemed the most desirable place in the world.

The train stopped twice to pick up more children. The first stop was at Wighton "Halt" where the platform was only long enough to take one carriage, and the second at Walsingham where correspondingly more children climbed aboard.

The fields in late Summer were a patchwork of sometimes unexpected colours. As well as the ubiquitous bleached barley, the richer gold of the oats and the coffee coloured wheat, there were fields of forget-me-not blue linseed, yellow mustard and, later in the war, scarlet poppies grown for opium. The government incentives for growing poppies were good, but my father never grew them as he was of the opinion that the soil would never be clear of them afterwards.

On arrival at Fakenham we streamed out on the mile long walk to the school, the older ones with the longer legs quickly taking the lead. We passed along the road where the cuckoo had given us his message and into the main shopping street of the town.

A cattle market was held regularly in the town and on market days cattle and sheep were driven through the streets to the market place making the streets and pavements alike their own. My father had on occasions bought bullocks in Fakenham market and driven them the 10 miles to Wells on foot through the various drovers' lanes.

One of the antique shops in the town was sometimes visited by Queen Mary during her visits to Sandringham and bore the sign *"By Appointment to..."* Inevitably the day had come when one of the bullocks being driven to market had broken loose and entered the open door of the shop, running amok. On being told of the incident, it was widely reported that Her Majesty had remarked that she had often heard of a bull in a china shop....

On arrival at school bewilderment set in with a vengeance. Gone was the security of one classroom for the whole day. Now each lesson seemed to demand a change of venue, the change heralded by an unseen electric bell. Endless books were handed out, all to be covered in brown paper, and a fresh begowned teacher appeared at every lesson. Obviously life from now on was going to be very different, and lessons were going to consist of much more than Shakespeare and French, but a start had been made. I was *"in"*.

CHAPTER SEVEN

 In the Autumn of 1939 the port was still functioning as usual. It was the busiest time of year for cargoes; first corn, and then sugar beet was loaded on to the visiting barges, and in return coal was brought in. The Quay was never a clean place on which to walk. The west end was usually thick with coal dust, and the rest would bear evidence of whatever cargo had been loaded last.

At this time of year as many as five or six barges together might be in the harbour, three alongside the Quay wall being loaded or unloaded, and the rest moored alongside them and waiting their turn, as the curve of the harbour wall would only accommodate three at a time. The barges could often be spotted on the horizon waiting for a tide big enough for them to cross the bar and sail into the harbour. On one occasion the *Alf Everard* missed her tide and had to anchor for a week off the bar before she could get in.

When one was seen, word would quickly spread, and any of us who were free would hurry to the Quayside to watch the arrival of the

Wells Quay, from the east end. Photo: Mark Woods

boat. With their huge brown sails extended they made an impressive sight gliding majestically by, the silence broken only by the slapping of water against their sides and the creaking of spars. Several of the barges were owned by F.T.Everard and Son of Greenhithe and were built at Great Yarmouth. The *Will Everard, Alf Everard, Ethel Everard* and *Fred Everard* were regular visitors and old friends.

Sometimes the deliveries were in the opposite direction, and the lifeboat *Silver Jubilee* was delivered to the Quayside by rail, by way of the branch line which ran through East End.

At this time all cargoes were unloaded manually. Railway wagons would be brought from the railway station along the branch line past the whelkhouses, and the engine would pull up at buffers just past Ship Cottage. The engine would then be uncoupled and returned to the station, while the trucks were pulled along the lines through the East End of the town along the road on to the Quayside by three horses, who delivered them to the west end of the Quay where coal was unloaded. The coal was brought from the hold of the boat in sacks carried on the backs of men, who had no protection but a split sack over their heads, and who carried it across a plank on to the quayside. From there they carried their sack up a ramp to be loaded on to the trucks, which were then dragged back to the coal yards at the East End of the town. There was nothing to separate the loaded wagons from pedestrians and other traffic as they made their journey down the centre of the road, but the horses' hooves and the clanking of the wagons gave plenty of warning of their approach.

In November and December sugar beet was brought in wagons from local farms to be unloaded and left in huge piles along the quayside, waiting for the barges which took it round the coast to the factories. The beet was lifted individually by hand, topped of its long tough leaves with a knife, and was coated in yellowish mud, which had a sweet sickly smell. The piles would sometimes lie on the Quay for days, and the greasy mud would creep further and further into the town. When the boat arrived the beet were tossed into the hold with shovels or forks.

At the east end of the Quay were granaries, tall like the maltings, and one having a chute which extended past the quay wall, and through which grain was sometimes passed straight into the hold of the waiting barge. But if the maltings were dark and mysterious, the granaries were bustling and extrovert. Their covered hoists unloaded the grain as it was brought from the farms, and the wheat was then either sent to the flour mill by the railway station or loaded on to the barges. The chute was not always used and most of the time the wheat was carried in sacks across the quay just as the coal had been, and then

The Old Maltings, now part of the community centre, Wells. Photo: Mark Woods

across a plank and deposited in the hold. Again the men wore sacks over their heads for protection and did the job at the double, the men turning and running back to the granary making way for the next runner, who was timed so that there should be no gap. As the tide rose or fell the boat rose or fell also, so that the angle of the planks gradually became more steep. Boats often came in with the tide, unloaded and departed with the next day's tide, and the port was popular because of the quick turn round.

There was no means of knowing that this was to be the end of an era. But as the war progressed, boats ceased to arrive at the Quayside. Increasingly grain and sugar beet were transported by lorry and the harbour channel, undisturbed by its former traffic gradually silted up more and more until, at low tide, it was possible to walk across it at some points. The only vessel in sight was an air/sea rescue boat which, together with the lifeboat, rescued many airmen forced down into the sea.

After the war had ended the channel was dredged and, slowly, boats returned. But the old methods had gone. The grain was now always loaded from the chute, and the hooded men were no longer needed. The sugar beet trade never returned, lorries having taken over the transport permanently.

Coal deliveries by boat also ceased with the war, the coal being delivered by train to the station, so that the line through the East End of the town fell into disuse. The rails remained embedded in the road for many years, but were eventually taken up and the scars hidden by tarmac.

Today's cargo is likely to be fertiliser, which can be unloaded by one man operating a crane. This was a cargo which would not have been needed before the war, when the farm animals provided all the manure necessary, and my father was very unpopular when he returned home after a day's muckspreading.

In his book *"Sailing Barges"*, F G C Carr tells us that from the outbreak of war the barges were not allowed to sail any further north than Yarmouth, although the *Will Everard* continued to carry cargoes between London and southern ports, sometimes coming under fire. The *Ethel Everard* was towed across to Dunkirk loaded with food, drinking water and ammunition, where she was beached and eventually destroyed.

Today many of the vessels moored at the Quayside are likely to be pleasure boats. The fronts of many of the granaries have been removed and the buildings turned into cafes and amusement arcades for the visitors who flock to the town in Summer.

Unloading the cargo at Wells quay, circa 1930. Photo: Eric Reading collection.

CHAPTER EIGHT

 Now the metamorphosis of Norfolk began. All over the county, but particularly along the coast, good arable land was torn up to construct army camps and airfields. The East coast would be in the front line of defence and preparations were made for invasion by Germany. The grass covered bank which acted as a sea defence, and which had been a favourite Sunday evening family walk, was blocked by successive barriers of barbed wire. At the end stood a sentry who inspected the permits which the fishermen now had to show before they were allowed to go to sea. The handles which started the engines on the fishing boats had to be taken home by the fishermen each evening so that the boats were immobilised. The soft white sand of the beach had been sown with mines, as had the cool pinewoods which backed the sand-dunes all along the coast. The cockle strands and winkle beds were no longer accessible and the neat line of beach huts, with names like *"Seagull"* and *"Rest-a-while"* had been stripped of their contents of deckchairs, spirit stoves, crockery and beach gear, and stood empty and deserted. As the war progressed storms tore off the roofs and doors and the huts filled with sand.

All along the coast from Weybourne to the Wash tubular scaffolding had been erected to prevent tanks landing. At the entrance to the harbour channel at Wells the small gap which had been left to allow the whelk boats through was not easy to find, especially as darkness approached.

This scaffolding remained in place throughout the war, but towards the end of hostilities when the wheel had turned full circle and the invasion had gone in the opposite direction, German prisoners of war were employed to dismantle the ugly erection. They worked on the beach all day, each of them carrying an identical lunch pack, and watching with interest while the lifeboat was launched. Later, when the lifeboat had returned, the Mechanic, Mr J Cox, noticed one of the prisoner's lunch packs inside the lifeboat house. A further search revealed one of the prisoners, and a plan to steal the lifeboat and sail it back to Germany was foiled.

Throughout the war the lifeboatmen had a rota for sleeping in the lifeboat house to be ready to go to the aid of aircrew in difficulties when returning from bombing raids over Europe. Later in the war when raids were carried out by 1,000 planes at a time, the door-knocker

Beach huts for the convenience of bathers along Wells beach.

Boats small and large, and the lifeboat house on the right, at the west end of the harbour.

of our house had to be permanently muffled with a duster as the constant vibration from the aircraft engines rattled it continuously. The whole county became a fortress and Wells took on the air of a garrison town. Soldiers and airmen, many of them from cities, crowded into the town from the surrounding camps, eager for entertainment and female company. The local girls had never had so much choice. Wells, with the only cinema for several miles around and a good supply of pubs, became the mecca for off duty servicemen, while the local boys were drafted elsewhere.

Aeroplanes, which had been rarely seen before the war, soon became commonplace. The few which had previously made an appearance at an Air Circus held just outside the town, seemed antiquated and pathetically slow in comparison with the Spitfires, Hurricanes, Wellingtons and Blenheims which had begun to criss-cross the coast.

To the East at Stiffkey and Weybourne anti-aircraft guns practised firing at a target towed by an Airspeed Oxford, which flew as far as Wells and then turned back, displaying the target all along the coast above the salt marshes. The crump of the guns was heard all day long in Wells.

The hours of darkness, which had previously been disturbed by little save the grinding rattle of the iron wheels of the night cart as it made its essential rounds, were now filled with the urgent bustle of troop movements. Soldiers frequently arrived in the town by train at night and piled into army lorries which rumbled away to the various army camps. The railway station which had formerly closed at 11p.m. after the arrival of the last train from Norwich, remained open into the night, and the banging of carriage doors, the clanking of meeting buffers and the hissing of the engines mingled with the shouting and singing of the soldiers, as they made their way to yet another uncomfortable camp. Sometimes a Scottish regiment passed through and I would stand in my garden in the darkness listening to the sad wail of the pipes and wondering what these highland men made of our coastal county.

In Wells, as in the rest of the country, there were other signs that times had changed, and us with them. Iron railings and gates had universally disappeared, taken, we were told, to make arms. We were also asked to donate old saucepans and frying pans for the same purpose. The newly installed air raid siren sounded its chilling warning, although as yet only for practice purposes.

There was a ban on movement on a 10 mile strip round the coast, and any unrecognised person asking for directions would be patriotically denied any help. Everywhere posters warned us against

"Careless Talk" and urged us to *"Dig for Victory"*. The street lamps were no longer lit, and blackout curtains or shutters prevented any light escaping from windows, or any fresh air from entering.

The Church Hall, which had been the venue for concerts, dances and parties, had been transformed into an emergency hospital to supplement the small Cottage Hospital. All the windows had been boarded up so that it was impossible to see in, but on one occasion when I passed and a door had been left open, the whole place seemed to be filled by scaffolding. I wondered where they would put the beds and the bedside cabinets and how people could breathe with no windows to open.

Rumours circulated throughout the area of attempts made by the Germans to land at various places along the coast. There was even a suggestion that a German submarine had been spotted off Holkham Bay. While there were always some people willing to believe these stories, the general consensus of opinion was that if you couldn't see it you shouldn't believe it. However, German E boats were certainly seen close to the coast by local fishermen.

About this time there was a casualty in the area. All vehicles abroad at night had heavily hooded headlights which let through only a narrow slit of light. A young dispatch rider travelling along the coast road towards Stiffkey at night was hit by an Army convoy coming in the opposite direction and killed. He was 20 years old and the town was shocked. Some 35 years later, my son and a friend, both keen motorcyclists, and the same age as the dispatch rider, returned to the area on holiday and camped at Stiffkey. Returning to their camp site in the evening they each experienced a feeling of unease and foreboding on passing the scene of the accident. At the time they had no knowledge of the dispatch rider's death.

But in 1939, a new way of life was opening up at school. The journey on the school train was apparently a bonus period for completing homework, and many *"tests"* were given and received during the 20 minute journey. Although we gave the engine drivers and guards nicknames, they were more on our side than we deserved, and I don't think anyone was ever allowed to miss the train on either the outward or return journey. The guard would go out of the station and scan all the approach roads for any stragglers and the engine driver would sound repeated warnings on his whistle before starting off.

On one occasion rumour went so far as to suggest that the king was going to pass the night in Wells station in the royal train. Why he should have wished to do so when only a few miles from the comfort of Sandringham remained a mystery, but there was certainly a very clean, new looking train, with blinds covering all the windows, left in the station all night, with an engine running. We were suitably impressed and boarded our train in unaccustomed and awed silence in the morning.

At school lessons were, on the whole, proving a satisfying challenge, but French looked like being a great disappointment. Although well into the term we had done little but learn to pronounce strange vowels through our noses. I was becoming very bored with *"arn"*, *"orn"* and *"urn"*. There had been an even worse disappointment in the English lessons. Shakespeare, I discovered to my dismay, was never read until the second year. Indeed the English mistress was of the opinion that it should not be read at all until the fourth year. There was some small comfort in the fact that the English mistress did not control the curriculum. The Biology and Chemistry Laboratories were places of absorbing interest, and the Chemistry Lab could be made to produce the most revolting smells by those sufficiently initiated, but the Physics Lab was a place of torture. I spent hours struggling with complicated Physics problems which made absolutely no sense to me at all and for which I could see no understandable reason. The answers to the problems were in the back of the text book and I resorted to multiplying or dividing by any number which transformed the question into something approaching the given answer, but all to no avail.

Later in the war a stray bomb fell in Fakenham churchyard. Luckily no-one was hurt, and no damage was done to the church, but that week we all had the opportunity to examine a real human skull in the Biology lesson. Perhaps it was fortunate that no local production of *"Hamlet"* was planned for that year.

Because of the belief that Hitler would attack with poison gas, some lessons had to be taken wearing gasmasks for practice. I hated the feel of the damp, clinging rubber and developed a fear that the strainer would become blocked and I would suffocate. I remember nothing of those lessons, save the misery of feeling I was experiencing my last moments on earth.

The situation at school was complicated by the evacuation of a boys' school from London to Fakenham which was to share the buildings with us during the day. Similar results have been made hilarious in the play *"The Happiest Days of Your Life"* but in real life events were much more frustrating. We took it in turns with the boys' school to use the school buildings, and when we were not in occupation, usually in the afternoons, had to walk in a crocodile to the local Church Hall, a quarter of a mile away, to do what we could there. The Hall was equipped with nothing but trestle tables and benches and most of the time was spent officially in reading our library books, or unofficially indulging in a game called *"Battleships"*.

Perhaps the most difficult time of all for me was during games and gym lessons. When athletic talent was handed out I was definitely the last in the queue, nor was I built for physical prowess. Indeed, a neighbour had once referred to me as *"a yard and a half of pump water"*. At Primary School games had mostly consisted of carrying bean bags and dumping them in buckets, a pastime at which even I could excell, but now there were the mysteries of hockey and netball to be divined. I tried, but there was always someone else yards ahead of me in control of the ball. However, there was one aspect of games lessons which I appreciated as much as anyone. The lane leading to the playing fields passed the caretaker's house where he had some prolific apple trees. Whenever any form was due for games, the caretaker, affectionately known as *"Taggles"* would stand behind his hedge and throw over armfuls of fruit for which we would scramble gratefully.

Unfortunately there was no such consolation before gym lessons. Why, oh why, could we not take our exercise safely on the ground? But we were expected to climb fearsome ropes and rope ladders and execute somersaults over vaulting horses. I had no ambition to become either a trapeze artist or a steeplejack and would willingly have risked being unhealthy if I could have avoided taking part, but pride prevented my saying anything and I remained the despair of the gym mistress.

The life boat slipway & quay 1900.

CHAPTER NINE

 The Thanksgiving for harvest was a very real one in Wells. With so much of the town's prosperity relying on the yield of both the land and the sea, a good harvest was indeed something for which to give thanks. The harvest of the sea was remembered in church with nets hung high in the west arch above the font, but the main decoration came from the land. No need here for packets of tea or tins of foreign fruit, the church overflowed with home grown produce. Potatoes scrubbed clean enough to eat, nestled next to highly polished apples. Piles of pears and plums were divided by marrows and punnets of runner beans. Tomatoes added a plenteous splash of colour, and, always, from the beak of the eagle on the lectern, hung a luscious bunch of purple grapes. The altar shone with giant spiky dahlias, and in front would be propped a life-sized sheaf of wheat made in bread. Among the beams in the roof of the nave 60 angels, their hands clasped in prayer gazed down benignly on the rejoicing congregation, while in the chancel 40 more, their instruments in their hands, were ready to assist the human choir below. To thee, O Lord, our hearts we did indeed raise.

Armistice Day, which arrived shortly afterwards, also held a special significance for everyone this year. The usual parade from the 1914-18 War Memorial to the church was swelled with contingents of soldiers and airmen from nearby camps as well as representatives from all the newly formed organisations. Practically everyone was involved in some form of Civil Defence, and although as yet uniforms were in short supply, steel helmets and armbands signified their allegiance. Even the youth of the town were represented by groups of Scouts, Girl Guides and Brownies.

At the service the *"Last Post"* reminded us that war was now as well as then, and the *"Reveille"* made its call for renewed effort. The packed congregation fervently sang the Jingoistic hymns supported by the belief that God and right were on our side, but still grateful for the protective barrier of the North Sea and the English Channel. After the service the parade reassembled and marched back to the War Memorial through the same streets which three months before had echoed to the music and laughter of the Carnival, but were now lined with more thoughtful spectators.

The excitement at the approach of Christmas was missing this year.

Many familiar faces had disappeared from the town as the men left to join the forces and their places were taken by older men, and, increasingly, women. Some of the boys who had dived from the Quay on summer evenings were now in the Royal Norfolk Regiment and would soon sail for Singapore, some never to return.

For several years previously the parish church had been the scene of a pageant held in the week after Christmas, at which the Christmas story was enacted. Most of the congregation took part in one way or another, and there was always room for another angel or shepherd as long as the actor could provide his own costume. In 1938 I had been chosen to play the part of the Virgin Mary as a child, probably because I had the ability to sit still. For this I assumed what I considered to be a suitably serious expression, until one of the angel choir suggested that perhaps it wasn't necessary to look quite so fierce. Thereafter I tried smiling, until told by a harassed Rector to remember that it was a serious occasion!. The Pageant was very popular, but 1938 saw the last one, at least for the time being.

The church itself had been built in 1460 in the Perpendicular style, but in 1879 during a severe storm lightning struck the eastern flank of the tower just below the belfry windows. It ran along the nave roof melting the lead and setting fire to the timbers. The church was completely gutted by the fire, but restored and rededicated in 1883. On the northern side of the church is a stained glass window portraying the Madonna and Child in the centre, flanked by St. Christopher and St. Nicholas, the patron saint of the church. If any stained glass was lost in the fire compensation is made by the brightness of light which pervades the church. In the churchyard is buried John Fryer, the Sailing Master of the *"Bounty"*, who survived the mutiny, although his stone is no longer decipherable, but other sailors are commemorated, some with their boats portrayed on their headstones.

The church bells, like all those in the land, had been silenced against the time when they might be needed to warn of an invasion. Not only could they no longer call the congregation to worship, but neither could they toll out the age of parishioners on their death.

Soon after Christmas the Northern Lights were seen in the sky over the Norfolk coast. This was an unusual, though not unique occurrence, and there was much discussion on the school train as to whether, as some said, this heralded a coming catastrophe for the country. However, my mother was of the opinion that it was more likely to mean that rough weather was on its way.

My mother's common sense was, as usual, on target. Gales roared along the coast bringing blizzards with them, and we awoke one morning to the eerie silence following the heaviest snowfall for many

The tower of St Nicholas church, Wells. Photo: Mark Woods

years. So severe had been the blizzard that a snowdrift extended some four feet inside our back door, forced through the cracks by the malevolent North-East wind. Outside the town the snow had filled the fields and roads alike to the height of the hedges and the whole area became one vast plain some eight or nine feet above the normal level of the ground. Trees buckled under the weight of snow and branches snapped. Along the roadsides drifts of snow reached as high as the telephone wires forming breaker like masses waiting to crash down on to the road beneath. Transport was possible by foot only and even the Army lorries could not bulldoze their way through. Work on the farm ceased, but the long walk along the top of the hedges had to be made each day to feed the stock. Chilblains sprouted like mushrooms and thoughts of invasion were pushed aside by more immediate problems. The town was cut off in all directions by road and the railway lines were blocked in Barsham Cutting. As this was between Wells and Fakenham, this successfully prevented our attendance at school. Old orange boxes were hurriedly knocked into sledges and everyone under 16 prepared to enjoy themselves.

The birds were not so fortunate. Their supplies of food had vanished beneath the snow and not a berry or a worm was visible.

Some had more ingenuity than others. The milk, which by now was being supplied in bottles, had usually been sampled by enterprising bluetits before it arrived. The other garden birds were forced to compete with screaming, bullying seagulls, which had been blown inland by the ferocity of the winds. They shrieked their demands for food at the very back doors of houses, while daily, stiff little feathered bodies were interred in fresh layers of snow. The shallow water in the harbour channel froze at low tide, and at high tide small ice floes could be seen floating in the water.

Soon it became apparent that there was to be no immediate respite and supplies in the town were beginning to run out. Snow ploughs were unknown, so the men of the town had to dig us out. With nothing but spades the work was carried out, more men joining in all the time. The digging continued over the days until a one vehicle track had been cleared along the main coast road, and inland along the Fakenham road, until eventually the diggers met up with their counterparts coming in the opposite direction from the next village.

But *"If Winter comes can Spring be far behind?"*

Eventually the thaw arrived and life began to return to normal. The melting snow flooded the fields so that Spring sowing had to be delayed, but by March it was possible for the cycle to begin again.

Easter was approaching and on Good Friday the new potatoes must be planted, as they had been for generations, although this year the church bells would not play *"Alleluia, sing to Jesus"* as the worshippers flocked to the services on Easter Sunday.

In spite of all the threats, Hitler had still not invaded, and although the situation in Europe was far from reassuring, Churchill's powerful oratory had produced a feeling of unity and resolution in the country. In North Norfolk *"We will fight them on the beaches"* had a very realistic ring.

At school things were looking decidedly brighter. As the prophesised raids on London had not materialised and everything there was peaceful, and possibly also because the situation in Norfolk was too peaceful, many of the boys from the evacuated school had returned home. Before long, so many had departed that the remainder were able to take their lessons in classrooms vacated for games lessons by those of us from the local school, and the curriculum returned to normal. Most of the male teachers had been called up and been replaced by mistresses or elderly parsons, but, to my personal relief, when the Physics master was called up no replacement could be found and the subject was temporarily dropped from the timetable.

French was becoming much more rewarding, and we could now string together complete sentences, convinced that our accents would pass muster, even in Paris. In English too, even in the absence of Shakespeare, there had been many rewards. We had made the acquaintance of Don Quixote and Sancho Panza, and the infuriating Dr Johnson, but, best of all in September we would be second formers, and then we would read *"Macbeth"*.

As I walked to the station each morning to catch the school train I watched the progress of the laburnum tree at the top of the hill. I had only recently learned its name and previously had always thought of it as the Golden Tree. Flowering trees and shrubs were not much in evidence in Norfolk then, all the garden space being used for the more practical purpose of growing vegetables, and this laburnum was the only one I had ever seen. It had always been a source of wonder, its bright beauty being so impractical, but as yet the branches and twigs remained bare and brown, with only the remnants of last year's seed pods clinging stubbornly on. But as the year progressed and the North East wind moderated I knew that inevitably the fairy gold must appear on the branches, and when the Midas-touched tree was in full bloom we could all be sure that the tide of Winter had turned.